MORE GEMS OF JAPANIZED ENGLISH

A further look at the
English-language follies and foibles
encountered in Japan

GW00634922

Miranda Kenrick

MORE GEMS OF JAPANIZED ENGLISH

illustrated by Herbie Naumann

YENBOOKS

YENBOOKS are published and distributed by
the Charles E. Tuttle Company, Inc.
of Rutland, Vermont & Tokyo, Japan
with editorial offices at
2-6 Suido 1-chome, Bunkyo-ku, Tokyo 112

LCC Card No. 92-80693
ISBN 0-8048-1854-1

First edition, 1992
Second printing, 1992

Printed in Japan

Contents

Foreword

THIRTY YEARS AGO the *Asahi Evening News,* one of Tokyo's daily English-language newspapers, invited its readers to send in photographs of their favorite examples of Japanized English. I think it offered ¥1,000 per contribution. The *Asahi* was so inundated with responses that, after a few weeks of publishing a captioned photograph a day, it discontinued the project. Had it continued, who knows? It might by now have been the paper's longest-running feature.

Fractured English has appeared in print for over one hundred years in Japan. The distinguished British scholar and writer Basil Hall Chamberlain, who first arrived in Japan in 1873, felt that his own collection of Japanized English deserved inclusion in his 1904 publication *Things Japanese,* a book that introduced the little-known country of Japan to the West.

I have lived in Tokyo all my life, and, like so many contemporaries as well as others before me, have laughed over countless examples of Japanized English. I could no more remember them after a day or two than I could remember a joke, so I formed the habit, as a schoolgirl, of copying down those that tickled me. In that spirit of "just for fun," I wrote an article in 1985 for the *Tokyo Weekender*. I had written several pieces before for other publications, and had also included many examples of my Japanized-English finds in a book called *Too Far East Too Long*.

The *Weekender* story I wrote triggered a surprisingly enthusiastic response. Many people sent the *Weekender* their own favorites, which the editor and publisher, Corky Alexander, passed on to me. My friends and acquaintances peppered me with their own finds. One article turned into a dozen, and a friend suggested weaving them into a book. Thus *Gems of Japanized English* came into being. As I was putting it together, I wondered why there hadn't already been several such books published. I understood the reason when I saw my lifetime collection put down on paper. Since Japanized English consists mostly of a garbled phrase or a wrongly used word or two, it takes a vast number of them to make a book. Without hoards of offerings from other people, there couldn't have been a *Gems of Japanized English*.

I still collect these "gems." And clearly so do other people or I would not have had enough material to fill a second book. I hope it entertains you as much as it does me.

Although I've never lived anywhere but Tokyo, I spend several months each year traveling. As I roam the world, I always zero in on written English wherever it may appear, be it on billboards, brochures, or menus. It's an ingrained response, but a harmless one that affords me considerable and continuing amusement. I realized long ago that Japan certainly has not cornered the market on quaint English. I have included in this book examples of humorous English from all over the globe. I did so for two reasons: first, I don't want you to think I'm picking on Japan, and second, all these other gems are just too good to keep to myself.

Without the contributions of friends and acquaintances, I wouldn't have had enough material for either volume of Japanized English. I cannot name each person, that would fill another book. However, I would like to thank Doreen Simmons, who has been a steady source of Japanized English as well as careless English spoken and written by native speakers. I would also like to thank Corky Alexander for his support over the years. Much of the material in this book has appeared in a different form in the *Weekender*.

—MIRANDA KENRICK

— 1 —
Wer-roo-come American Libation Forces

WHEN THE ALLIES' occupation of Japan began immediately after the end of World War II in 1945, many within the Occupation forces must have wondered what lay ahead. How would the defeated nation receive them? With hostility? Sabotage? Could they hope for anything more than sullen, resentful cooperation?

Probably few people could have predicted the future, yet from the beginning the Japanese attitude was positive. This sign, at the entrance of a "biru haw-roo" (beer hall), said it all. In clear, Japanized English, it beamed: "Wer-roo-come American Libation Forces." And welcome they were.

Japan had initially, and reluctantly, opened its doors to the world in the mid-nineteenth century. By the turn of the century, Japanese hotels, restaurants, and shops were printing brochures, menus, and advertisements in rather strange English.

During the Occupation years, however, copywriters outdid themselves, both in volume and quixotry. Westerners did doubletakes, then often photographed or wrote down the mangled phrases. The English used in Japan today isn't nearly as fractured as it once was. Collecting what examples there are, though, remains a hobby of visitors and residents alike.

Immediately postwar Occupation wives had their hair done at "Clean and Most Sonorous Booty Shop," while their husbands might have patronized barbers calling themselves "New Hair Dizain Shop."

In those early years, when labor was cheap, many a foreign wife had her favorite neighborhood "dress maka." Her husband could frequent establishments such as "Lucky Tailor" that offered "highest technic, lowest fare and punctual promise." One "high class tailor" declared that he "serves for American that depends on your fancy," while another offered "New and Old Clothes Fixed Civilized Style." One enterprising tailor expanded his work to interior decoration. His shop bore the legend: "Dress Your Mroo With Beautiful Drapery."

In the days before television was a part of every

NEW SECOND HAND BOOKS

household, bookshops sprouted up around the city. One shop even offered English-language volumes. Its sign said: "selling, buying New Second-Hand Books." Odds and ends could be purchased either from the startlingly named "Sun Light Soap Lever Brothels Ltd," or another establishment grandly calling itself "Delucks."

Clocks and watches were restored at "watches ripear." A shop selling matresses, quilts, and blankets called itself a "sleeping shop," while a paper hanger specialized in "A Paper Hunger, A Sliding Door, A Faiding Screen, A Picture Frame, A Wall Pasting."

One English-language map of the time showed a very different Tokyo from the city of today. The map pinpointed a spot near Tokyo Bay and

identified it as a "Dirty Water Punishment Place."
Somehow, in translation, the Japanese for sewage
disposal plant metamorphosed into "Dirty Water
Punishment Place."

✳ ✳ ✳

Since the majority of drivers in Occupied Japan
were Americans, it stood to reason that traffic signs
should appear in English. Gas stations sold "Ga So
Rin" and traffic instructions included:

> SULOW
> No Paking Zone
> Tool Load Intrance

Load Closed
Stop: Drive Sideways

A road sign near Grant Heights, an American base outside central Tokyo, said: "NO VEHICLES THROUGH after about 3 km. drive on the left way to right. Then you may Meet This Road at Taishido." Then again, many a driver may not have.

Military bases, of course, were communities complete unto themselves. Army buses transported school-age children. On the back of each school bus was the standard American injunction "STOP— THEN PROCEED WITH CAUTION." In the early fifties, local Tokyo buses crisscrossing the city adopted that excellent maxim. There was, however, a difference between the signs on the American and Japanese buses. The Japanese buses forgot the word STOP. A popular truck and car bumper sticker tried to help, though, by commanding "No Kiss."

By the late fifties and early sixties there were enough vehicles on the road to warrant "traffic safety weeks." Out came the banners to be hoisted over major roads. They read: "PRAY—SAFETY—TRAFFIC."

Of course, there were also signs at train stations. One on the platform of a major station said: "First Class Car stops here (in case of 12 car consist)." Eventually "12 car train" replaced "12 car consist."

Meanwhile, a restaurant at the Tokyo international airport put up this well-meaning sign: "Any of your suggestions or complaints, you would kindly hear us." The men's restroom, also at the airport, had this helpful notice: "Stepping on button to operating. Rub hands lightly and rapidly. To dry face turn nozzel up. Lift up foot to stop."

Even Tokyo's zoos had signs in English. One requested visitors "don't fee animals" and ordered "No smoking afire on this way ahead within 10 km." Another had a more cryptic sign: "Numbers of pens snow best course." It's likely that "snow" was meant to be "show" and each animal pen had a number which visitors could follow.

I nominate the next set of directions as the best for summing up the glorious confusion of Tokyo during the first few decades after the war. A restaurant printed its own map to guide customers through the labyrinth of Tokyo streets. The map had directions printed on it, in careful English: "Turn to your left (right) in front of frower shop."

— 2 —
Burn Pond & Sulphor

THIS IS AN example of the kind of document frequently received at the headquarters of the Supreme Commander of the Allied Powers (SCAP). The letter was written by idealists wanting to launch a "No Lie Party."

PETITION OF "NO LIE PARTY"
(Uso Iwanu Kai)

Dagrass Mackather

Dear Sir!

Petition:-

We named "No Lie Party" has born at Numazu City, Shizuoka Prefecture, fine landscape the foot of picturesque Mt. Fuji. This party is consulting with Mayor and chief member of Public Peace Committee at Numazu or others, & on back of Numazu Christian Party. The members of "No Lie Party" are not only Japanese, but foreiner at any province in this world as if "Rotary-Club" & make up friendship, to trade every and then exchange the Tourist party etc. The spirit is same as Christism, included personal or international love. At any rate now happens bloody affairs about every days & dark and darker and the statements or leads of our Goverment as if no effect and people put on unsafty, such anxious has begin to this plan.

We, premirily, are not religionor or holyer & only

business men, however must keep "lie no tell", holding good interview in members. This shall give great "Mesu" in Japan, if our idea can realize in world, visit eternal peace to every states & no necessary "The International League of Peace", but such an idea not soon, so we wish get members, by & by, & larger & larger.

Dear Sir!

Can you permit this plan as one of your good conducts in now Japan? Pleas give us all approval & O.K. as soon as possible. We believe that this plan is big tock in Japan, if you please give us O.K.

yours sincerely
S. Ito
K. Suzuki

Mach 1948

"Notice" we think

In case permit colonize, such a circle shall be get specialy.

"Bible" teach us.

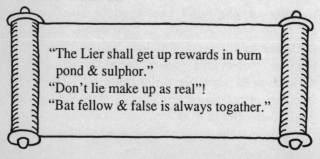

"The Lier shall get up rewards in burn
pond & sulphor."
"Don't lie make up as real"!
"Bat fellow & false is always togather."

Alas, the story ends there. The history of the Occupation contains no footnote on the "No Lie Party," nor do we know what happened to the men who wanted to organize it.

*   *   *

About the same time, an American diplomat in Tokyo addressed the students of an English-language school. The girls were high school students, keen to master English. A few days passed. Then one of the students visited the American's office to deliver an original present. The girls had put their heads together and written a poem which they dedicated to the diplomat. It read:

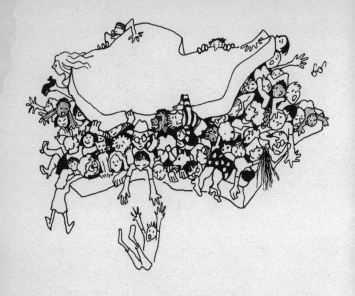

The Sky is Blue,
The Earth is Green,
We are all Sandwiched
In between.

*   *   *

The Japanese have long had a propensity for adopting foreign words and making them their own. German, Portuguese, English; no need to be fussy. However, I can offer examples only of words that I recognize as having been born English.

Here are a few Occupation-day samples. A stationery shop called itself "noto bukku," a bar named itself "wandufaru," and a coffee shop was known as "coffee and boozu." A footwear shop became a "shiuzu shop." A pachinko parlor—the Japanese craze for pinball machines goes back many a year—emblazoned its entrance with the word "HOMURAN." The owners seemed to want customers to think they'd hit home runs within. A schoolgirls' band had "guides bando" written on their drums. A photographer offered to take portraits. His shop was called "potoreto shutagio."

*   *   *

To this day, cash is king in Japan. Is this perhaps the only country in the world where people walk about daily with huge sums of money in their pockets? Somehow, paying by check has not yet caught on. Not that banks haven't tried. Several decades ago, one launched a campaign to promote the use of checkbooks. The campaign slogan was "Life in Check." It was supposed to be obvious from those three words that paying by check would ensure good living.

Another advertisement from the fifties was for a versatile lotion. It read: "Tired Aching Feet Gives Prompt Relief After Shaving Cooling Smoothing." Clearly—it's perfectly clear, isn't it?—the lotion gave prompt relief to tired, aching feet, and was also cool and soothing for newly shaven faces.

Then there is the hair cream called "Xebec" whose use "makes your hair shiny-crean. A marvelous ingredient in Xebec will impart your hair nourishing and natural brilliance and also Xebec give out elegantic smell." Aaaahhh.

A fashion advertisement in Japanese praised the color of the clothes it was promoting as "wonderful beyond words or thought." Unfortunately, the words chosen to give the slogan a little zing in English were "Unthinkable Color Combination."

A bar called itself "Bar Sun Raise," which prompted the question—did it mean to be sun rise or sun rays? Not that it would have made a dramatic difference.

Finally, a Tokyo beer hall identified itself as "Beer Hall For Allied Persnels From P.M. 4 till At 7. Pacifk Ocean Club." Perhaps it served a special of the time, an American whiskey that was advertised as "Old American Whiskey—Established 1492."

— 3 —
...And They All
Bowed Back...

THERE ARE SOME things you cannot imagine ever changing in Japan: bowing, for instance. It's difficult to realize how unconsciously you have adopted the habit until you catch yourself bowing to someone at the other end of the telephone line.

I once had a post-office box in a very small post office. The row of boxes was on the customer side of the counter, and mine happened to be on the very bottom level. Usually I squatted down to see if there was any mail. One day, however, I bent over to look. As I straightened up, I happened to glance over the counter. All the post-office workers were on their feet, politely bowing back at me.

In 1990, Tokyo's celebrated Imperial Hotel commemorated its hundredth anniversary. In these one hundred years it has been rebuilt and expanded a number of times. The famous Frank Lloyd Wright-designed building opened on September 1, 1923. Would you believe that the Great Kanto Earthquake struck during the opening ceremonies? The Imperial Hotel withstood the shocks that devastated much of Yokohama and Tokyo, and sheltered guests and Tokyo residents alike for the first few days after the earthquake.

An American businessman chose to stay in the Imperial on his first trip to Japan in 1959. After settling into his room, he went down to the tobacco counter in the lobby and asked, "What kind of cigarettes do you have?"

The girl behind the counter smiled at him and replied, "Peace and Hope."

The man blinked. Then he pulled himself together and said, "Well! That's very nice of you and I wish you all the best, too. But what kind of cigarettes do you have?"

Not until he was shown the packages did he realize that Peace and Hope were brand names of cigarettes. He told the story over and over, chuckling anew with each recap. "Can you imagine cigarettes being called Peace and Hope?" he used to say.

*   *   *

Something I hope will never change in Japan is the helpfulness of the average person. If you're caught in the rain, someone will most likely hold an umbrella over you. Ask for directions, and as often as not you'll be escorted to your destination. Department stores and shops think nothing of delivering on Sundays or after hours. We take for granted that we will eventually be reunited with wallets or valuables, contents intact, after carelessly leaving them behind on trains or in taxis.

An American woman even received this useful advice when her visa was due for renewal and she wanted to change her status in Japan. A government official, no less, told her, "Go to immigration before your visa explodes." Which she did, and it didn't.

Here is another "only in Japan" story. We were at lunch in the Capitol Tokyu Hotel. A firm favorite of residents and visitors alike, the Capitol is famed for its personalized service.

So there we sat at the monthly luncheon of a ladies' charitable organization. It was a set lunch, but we asked the young waiter if we could possibly have rye bread instead of white. Worry clouded his face, then off he trotted. He did not reappear, and by the time dessert arrived, we had forgotten about the bread.

As the coffee cups were being cleared and we settled back to listen to the speeches, the waiter reappeared. Very quietly he placed a prettily wrapped box on the table, then retreated. The box contained half a loaf of rye bread.

My friend Judy, also at a set dinner, this one in the Tokyo Foreign Correspondents Club, asked the waiter if she could take home her lambchop bones for her dog. He, too, looked somewhat disconcerted.

As Judy left the table after dinner, the waiter was hovering in the doorway. He presented her with two large shopping bags, filled with lambchop bones. Yes, he'd whipped around the kitchen, collecting every bone from every plate.

Judy's dog was happy for a month.

∗　　∗　　∗

A resident businessman was entertaining overseas visitors at lunch in the Keyaki Grill, the Capitol Tokyu's most elegant restaurant. When it came time to pay the bill, he gave the waiter a credit card.

After an unusual delay, the waiter returned to the table empty-handed. He looked harried and whispered, "Very sorry, sir, but we cannot return your card."

"Why ever not?" demanded the man. "I need it!"

"Yes, sir. Very sorry, sir. We dropped it, sir. We will return it to your office later, sir."

The card had slipped out of the waiter's hand and disappeared underneath the floor-to-ceiling wine rack. The rack had to be completely dismantled before the card could be retrieved.

Later that afternoon, the secretary's buzz announced visitors. Into the businessman's office, single file, marched three tuxedoed waiters. The first carried the offending card and bill on a silver salver. It had yet to be signed for the lunch. Waiter Number Two carried the apology, in the shape of a large box of cookies. Waiter Number Three carried nothing, he was keeping the others company. The bill was signed, apologies were repeated, and the waiters backed out. Just another day in the life of a Tokyo waiter.

Back in the seventies, a longtime British resident of Tokyo made up his mind that he would retire on New Year's Eve, 1999. One night, having had one too many, he phoned his favorite Tokyo hotel and said that he would like to make a reservation for a party on December 31, 1999.

Long pause. Then the courteous voice at the other end of the telephone replied, "I think we are very busy on that night. How about December 30?"

*   *   *

Sometimes the very best of intentions can reach the most muddled of conclusions. About a decade ago, a Tokyo shop decided to outdo all its competitors with its Christmas spirit. Sure enough, you'd never seen a larger decoration. A giant cross dominated the outside of the building. And who should be crucified on it but Santa Claus!

— 4 —
Don't Close Your Face to Monkies

"DISCOVER JAPANESE PEOPLE Alive in Their Festivals," says the advertisement for a book on festivals, put out by none other than the Japan Travel Bureau. It's a recent publication, too, which prompts the question—why aren't native speakers employed to ferret out such blunders?

The question has been asked for decades, and certainly must have been asked in the early postwar years at the time of publication of an official guide to the Grand Shrine at Ise. The Grand Shrine is one of Japan's finest examples of architecture, a sacred shrine where Shinto traditions have long been faithfully observed.

Believe it or not, the brochure to which I am referring said, "The Ise Ground Shrine here dedicated to Amaterasu Omikami a goddess who was the central figure of the God Age in Japan is revered as a mental home of the Japanese people."

Speculation about the translation is useless. How long could it have been before the proper authorities were notified? How many copies of the brochure were hastily recalled and destroyed? Of course, plenty of them must have slipped through the cracks.

*   *   *

Nara is one of Japan's ancient capital cities. One of its main tourist attractions is Horyuji, the oldest temple in Japan and one of the oldest wooden buildings in the world.

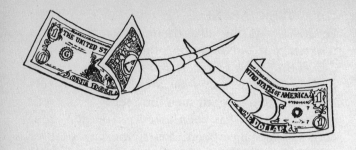

Nara is also famous for its large deer park. A placard placed prominently in the park during the Occupation days said: "Beware of Bucks With Long Horns." That sign disappeared many years ago, more's the pity. However, errors still creep into Nara's English-language publications. Quite recently a cultural asset was labeled a "fork museum." Perhaps "folk" might have been the word of choice.

Neighboring Nara is Kyoto, also a former Japanese capital city, and still a town of old-world charm with its temples and shrines. Its many places of historic interest warranted brochures in English for the benefit of Western visitors. Sometimes, however, a tourist didn't necessarily know much more about a place after reading the brochure. For instance, a pamphlet on the Katsura Imperial Villa once said:

There are several pavillions around the pond and the connecting paths, along which various phases of landscape defelope: mountains, rivers, fields, inlets beaches and all that. Not only the changes in sight, but also delightful changes in touch to the foot occur everywhere on the paths, because of the variety of surfacing materials.

Although the printed English word in Japan is usually flowery, sometimes to an extreme, the odd pamphlet produces extremely bland prose. One might wonder why this should be so in Kyoto guidebooks, for Kyoto, of all places, justifies

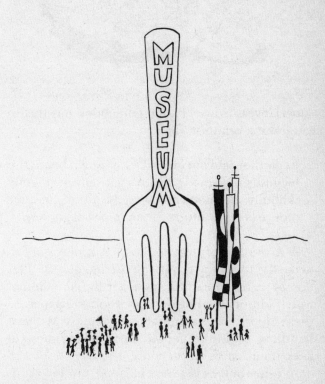

superlatives. However, one guidebook has this to say about a beautiful villa:

> Its garden, laid out in the 17th century, boasts the biggest scale among Kyoto's gardens. Its dignity skillfully harmonized with beautiful mother nature is really fitting for an imperial garden.

A Kyoto inn of bygone days felt it necessary to make the following request to foreign guests: "Ples do not toghch the wols." It was a truly old building, with traditional sliding doors of wood and paper. As these doors were vulnerable to clumsy Western handling, the innkeeper was simply asking guests to keep their hands off the walls.

Another hotel, elsewhere in Japan, proffered this

information about regulating the air conditioning in the guest rooms: "Cooles and Heates: If you want just condition of warm in your room, please control yourself."

A third hotel asked its guests to "hand over their car key to car taker," while another posted this sign: "Plese. Silently Walk Go."

Still another hotel, in its printed notes "for the safeguard of the guests," said: "Be careful. Never leave open the door full and a half."

There's a sign by an escalator in a luxurious, ultramodern, Western-style Tokyo hotel that says: "Notice. please keep aware of your dress be-nip-in by escalator." You have been warned.

*　　*　　*

PLES DO NOT TOGHCH THE WOLS!

COOLES AND HEATES:
If you want just condition of warm
in your room, please control yourself.

Someone once told me that his favorite example of Japanized English was a sign on Mt. Takao, a day's outing from Tokyo. It was an admonition to foreigners not to "open their faces to monkies" lest they make the monkeys feel menaced.

However, the rules and regulations of the Takao Mountain Railway Company's Japan Wild Monkeys Protection Club have since come my way, and it would seem that I was misinformed. You may open your face to monkeys. That's perfectly acceptable, and quite safe. What you should avoid, however, is closing your face to them.

Here is the notice from the Mt. Takao Monkey Observation area:

RULES TO KEEP IN THIS PLACE

We call this "MONKEY PALADISE" because more than thirty monkies are left free in this place.
These monkies live accoring sich to their wild nature since they are kept for ecological observation purpose, even.
Please keep the following rules in order to prevent accidents caused by offensive threatments against monkie nature.
We cannot be responsible for your accidents happened by disregarding these rules.

LET'S OBEY INSTRUCTIONS IN CHARGE AND KEEP FIVE POINT

1. Don't touch monkies
   If you do, they will bite or scratch you, mis-understanding that you are going to catch.
2. Don't close your face to monkies.
   For monkies, closing face means "threat"
3. Don't tease monkies
   They will be mad and pounce on you if you pat or shout
4. Don't show your fruits,
   If you do so, they will steal from you, thinking you have brought food for them.
5. Don't leave younger children walk about alone.

*　*　*

— 5 —
Walking Closets

EVEN IF YOU don't drive a "Rose Royce," you need a parking space for your car. As a matter of fact, space is such a problem in Japan that you must prove you have a legal parking spot before you're allowed to buy a car.

Things weren't always like this. During the Tokyo Olympic games in 1964, when the city was bending over backwards to be accommodating and hospitable, two curb signs appeared on opposite sides of a downtown street. "No parking," said one sign. Well, that's to be expected. On the other side, however, was the amiable "May parking."

Can you imagine finding such a sign on a Tokyo street today? Legal parking spaces are scarce and seldom available, while parking lots are usually crammed full.

Dire warnings sometimes appear. A small private parking lot in a residential neighborhood in central

Tokyo posted the usual prohibitions about illegal parking, in English. It went on, however, to say: "Besides the above fine. Tires will be flattened." Furthermore, "No trespassing: Police will be called in to arrest intruders. No littering. This is not a toilet for dogs. Dogs with or without owners will be regarded as intruders." Point taken!

On the subject of cars, a friend whose truth-telling I have no reason to doubt assured me that there was once—and who knows, perhaps there still is—an antifreeze spray called "Hot Piss."

Perhaps the same genius was responsible for labeling moist hand towels "Cat Wetty. For your car life." If it was the same man, he seems to have had a one-track mind.

*   *   *

Some years ago, residents of a housing compound in Tokyo received a circularized letter. It was from the management, thanking the tenants for their patience during the installation of a new sewage system. It read: "We appreciate that you make use of our compound house. By the way, as of a sewage construction, although we made you inconvenience of your life during under construction of sewage, we had completely finished the sewerage construction and could discharge without any trouble for your cooperation. We would like to thank you for your cooperaton."

Signs in English are regularly posted in apartment buildings with Western occupants. Some are permanent, like this one in an elevator: "Please keep the finger away from the button that is unnecessary to you."

Some signs have a short life span. This one is an autumn special: "You are warned of splinkling trees with insecticide."

During a water shortage, a sign that said "No using for stopping of a flow" perplexed even those who knew that water needed conserving.

Water shortage or not, it's advisable nowadays to filter tap water. An advertisement for a water-purifying machine proclaimed: "Ample of safe and

tasty water is guaranteed for you!" And recommended itself for "maintaining healthy for oversea company staffs." Among its selling points, it promised to "remove all water fur, madness and odor."

So now that your water is free of fur, madness, and odor, you're ready for coffee. Whether or not you're ready for a certain coffee grinder, however, is a different matter. The grinder in question says of itself: "You can't afford to grind grains while having coffee itself & enjoying hand works to powder, befited to lay is the wooden item of interior at anywhere want too . . . Coffee fragrances matches to the article in a cute and quiet circumstance. Daily sweat is nullified by this admirable coffee set at free chatting."

*　　*　　*

You never know what you might find in your letter box. Perhaps a note from a neighbor who has accepted a package on your behalf saying: "Go to Mr. Goto house and catch. Neighbor house."

Or perhaps an advertisement for a mail-order catalog called "Catch eye! Catalog shopping."

Or you might find pamphlets offering houses and apartments "too lent." One company promotes Kugahara, a suburb of Tokyo, as a "tranquil town," going on to say:

This region is the admiration of people. It have a

CATCH EYE!
CATALOG SHOPPING

high level of culture. There is calm about Kugahara and a lively strength of future lies hidden in there. There assert affluent life and the social status of people who live in there. Kugahara is full of verdure on the fragrant breeze.

Another company offers another area, Meguro, as an "excellent location makes your daily life thrilling and fascinating." The apartment on the market has "all sides well-lighted room plan by taking fully advantage of the natural conditions such as sunlight and wind." The floor plan shows the master bedroom, with bathroom en suite, plus a "walking closet." Now that really opens up possibilities for a thrilling life. Imagine your closets standing up and moving around!

Another house is recommended because it is

near a "pound" and has a "parch." The enclosed map clears up the "pound" mystery, for the house is within walking distance of an attractive pond. The floor plan shows a porch outside a living room.

*   *   *

Moving is an inevitable part of expatriate life. People who move regularly say that it is sometimes easier to cross the world than to move across a large city. At least moving companies in Tokyo generally maintain high standards and you can expect your possessions to reach their destination intact, whether they are traveling near or far. Boxes are all labeled properly with such identifying marks as "badroom," "cluss" (clothes), and "long shoes" (boots).

A family leaving Japan is required to fill out a lengthy inventory form. The bedroom items to be listed include sheets, pillows, blankets, and "quits." By the time the wife has cleared out all her closets—although they obligingly stand still—she is well and truly ready to call it quits.

— 6 —
Let's Burning Your Body

THE BILLBOARD HAS a picture of a ballerina. In English are the words "Shape up Studio." So far, so good, but the next slogan is the startling "Let's Burning Your Body." Well, I don't know about you, but I'd think twice about offering my body to be burned.

Then there's the "body cation studio" and the "face cation studio." Line them up with the "studio fits" aerobics class, and you may well wonder what goes on behind closed doors in Japan.

Certainly you marvel at the sheer originality of the names of services, shops, and products. "Wedding Mama" is a bridal advisory service, while a well-known wedding hall is called "Green and Human Plaza." I suppose that's where brides go for "My Pure Wedding," as advertised on posters.

A window has these words in English on it: "Cut Space. For man with Ladys." It's a barber-cum-hairdresser, in case you're puzzled. You could well have supposed it to be a hospital!

Kiosks on train platforms that sell newspapers, magazines, candy, gum, and cigarettes have "Let's Kiosk" emblazoned on them.

A moving van has the following logo plastered over its vehicles: "Moving My Staff." You know perfectly well that their staff moves your stuff, but the logo still gives you pause.

The advertisement for a store called "Funny Ornament" attracts your attention. What "Funny Brand" items could it be selling? Lo, they are merely "cosmetic things and many variety goods, for example: hair brush, comb, cosmetic bag . . . etc." The advertisement goes on to claim: "The Best Quality and Best Design. We can receive your order smoothly and kindly!!"

A department-store counter of soaps, oils, and lotions is called "Happy Bath Day." It displays

---

Cosmetic Things & Many Variety Goods
For example: Hair Brush, Comb, Cosmetic Bag...etc.

The Best Quality and the Best Design
We can receive your order smoothly and kindly!!

FUNNY BRAND **Funny Ornament Co., Ltd.**

scrubbing brushes of different sizes that are designed to attend to different parts of the anatomy. The brushes have labels attached to them, with phrases in English. The messages say such things as "First Body Care. Keep your body conditioned well with pure mind," "Sensible your life on the brushes," and "This brush is named Avanty beauty body brush. For your beauty and charmy life."

Another counter in the shop, filled with face powder, eye shadow, and mascara, is called "Kiss Me." Next to it is a counter covered with nail polish and lipstick. It is called "Lovely Match."

You can buy eye shadow in Japan called "fit net," and there are entire ranges of makeup with names such as "Cookie-face" and "Salad girl." No limit to new images! To top off your new look, splash on a perfume "for your olfactory."

"Juicy Pot" and "Ku Ku Boutique" are clothing stores. Ku Ku Boutique goes on to describe itself as catering to "fashion affected ladies." Well, perhaps some folk justify being so labeled.

*　　*　　*

A florist in a country town has a "Flower Communication" message on a plaque outside the shop. It says: "The flowers in recollection sing a poem in sepia color. Time seems to return to the twin of it's beautiful melody flow. Please listen to the dream a fresh heart discloses. Please look at my fresh face. Please receive it just when you open your heart. A bouquet to all of you over the world."

An electronic-goods shop window features a poster of two young Japanese women. There they smile, two ordinarily pretty young faces. However, the writing on the poster is anything but ordinary. It says:

WJNK

An angel is scribbling on the sky blue canvas. Their reflections like waves where mermaids remeet. Love is like a rainbow in seven magical colors. A saran-wrapped kiss tasting of apples.

The sheer originality of the message rates a gold star, even if its meaning is unintelligible.

A department store recently displayed this sign in one of its windows:

> It must be tenderness given by those close to them that lessen their loneliness and relieve them of their unwilling reserve to the people around them encouraging them to continue to live.

I think I understand that one. Live on, everyone!

A poster of a young Audrey Hepburn as she appeared in the film *Roman Holiday* once graced the wall of the computer corner of a small department store. You might wonder why it was with the computers. The writing on the poster said: "A Lover's Posy. How do you say in French 'my brother has a lovely girl' and . . . 'I wish I were my brother.' An amorous elegant and cheerful of a gentleman and a lady." Whatever would Miss Hepburn think?

There are slogans that remain incomprehensible, no matter how much you analyze them. A calendar with the message "skin clock for those wishing to become a dog," for one. What about "tissue of puppies" and "tissue of kittens" on tissue boxes? Or a clock with "lay or bust" on its face?

How did toilet paper come by its name "Naive

Lady"? At least toothpaste being transformed into "tooth pasty" is more easily understandable.

A packet of drinking straws is called "Maybe." The fine print reads:

> This is convenient and useful shape you can combine colors cheerfully. Maybe is frank goods by your sense and idea. You have various uses one after another.

Such as what, you may well ask. A drinking straw is a drinking straw!

There are "bellpaint" and "bellpint" pens on sale in Japan. Yes, there are ballpoint pens, too. A pocket flashlight is "neatly for, brightly and long use, nice oberlite." A storage case is labeled "pastel tone box for casual life communication."

A gift catalog includes a choice item called "Mr. Uncle Chimney." The blurb says: "I am glad to see you in 'Santa World.' A fairy tale of Christmas father. His name is 'Uncle Chimney.' Please enjoy yourself. Santa Claus Story."

maybe

THIS IS CONVENIENT AND USEFUL SHAPE YOU CAN COMBINE COLORS CHEE- RFULLY. MAYBE IS FRANK GOODS BY YOUR SENSE AND IDEA. YOU HAVE VA- RIOUS USES ONE AFTER ANOTHER.

A toy shop has a "Non-Toxic Non-Edible Magic Chameleon's Tongue, Wild Animated Tongue Will Shock You Greatly!" The chameleon's tongue comes complete with this message:

> The product has stickiness, it can be stretched like soft rubber and will stick things like stick-fast glue. It is a game to play with sticking things from far away.

The cautions include:

> Do not throw toward head or face of person. Do not throw toward or put near the fireplace. Though not toxic, it is forbidden to eat. Do not overstretch the tongue of the Chameleon, otherwise, it will go off.

Then there's a "Super Skiing Penguin" that has this label attached to the model:

Dear customer:

As a cleanly creature, penguins may get ill and refuse to ski when constant operations cause dust. Take care of your cute friends as below and you would share the incredible joy of their race . . . Penguins will become crippled when forced to ski on the floor.

— 7 —
Soft as a Baby's Arse

THERE IS AN advertisement for a dictionary available in Japan that says:

> Possibly the best dictionaly availbel—is the World Book Dictionaly . . . Its fromat and definitions are superb, its coverage broad and its introductory material outstanding in quality and readability.

All very well and fine, but what about its spelling?

Sometimes, when Japanese copywriters are creating catch phrases in English, they are told exactly how many words to use. What's more, those words must be of specified length. That explanation could account for the riveting commercial for tissue paper that claims to be "soft as a baby's arse." Well, why not? Soft as a baby's bottom is perfectly acceptable, but apparently the copywriter was looking for a shorter word. So he consulted his trusty dictionary and found a synonym with just the right number of letters.

The dictionary is also responsible for the choice of the word "organ" in this caption chosen for *Phantom of the Opera* T-shirts: "She chased him around the opera house and caught him by the organ." The person who decided on that sentence couldn't understand the uproar he had created. He brought out his dictionary and there was the definition, proper and correct, of the musical instrument found in cathedrals.

An American copywriter is required to rewrite the following Japanized-English copy for "Oraview," a piece of oral-hygiene equipment. Were he not able to read the original Japanese, he says he couldn't have done this job:

1. Irradiation magnifying glass for the mouth.
2. The right care of the mouth starts to see it. "Hukuba oraview" is a pocket equipment which is deviced to see all the mouth by myself personally. In order to advance the brushing skill and detect an abnormal in its early stages, and makes good use of it at home.
3. The combination of enlarged mirror and dental mirror can be reflected on the surface and reverse side. Dental mirror is oscillating revolution type and can be moved to the spot with complete control. Can be seen the shady point exactly with the light. Can be use of checking buss, nostril and eyeball except tooth. Easy for taking care of it because washing in water without using soap totality. Dental mirror can be sterilized by boiling and a medical fluid.
4. Oraview is making habitual use of the world.
5. Set a dying lock. Sordes on a tooth are colored with red by a dying lock. This is caused by halitosis, a decayed tooth and pyorrhea. Take preventive measures against the disease of tooth without leaving brush of tooth.

You can't help but wonder who wrote the copy for a cleansing cream that "Cleans up your act by cleaning out your pores." In the same store, you might find a hair pomade with the following copy written on its jar:

'Reims' has that modern stickiness because it is made from botanical oil. Of course it is very easy to take down oil with shampoo. Well, then 'Reims' has elegant glosenest has fragrance-etc, there factors are non-comparably fine with other pomade. Don't hesitate, try 'Reims' once! If had not her fine truly is the culmination of beauty. And it is a eternal truth for us. Have you the hair as the culmination of beauty? Don't be pessimistic! Voila 'Reims' 'Reims' 'Reims'! As you know our hair is stiff so it is necessary the pomade which has moderate stickness to settle it.

A lengthy news release comes from a beauty shop telling us that "one of the most unstable problems for foreign residents in Japan, especially for ladies, is not able to make themselves understood in a beauty salon. For the foreign ladies to enjoy more of their happy and comfortable life in Japan, such a beauty shop is required as to make better understanding of those ladies with strong self-assertion and provide service suitable for their individuality."

The news release goes on with a flourish: "Whether or not the hair style finishing that satisfies them can be obtained in a beauty salon in a foreign country where a language is not well understandable—this will cause them to be very uneasy about their own hair style making. For driving away their feeling of unrest, and providing satisfactory hair style to them, we, staff members are working hard at our English conversation so that we can explain any details on hair style making, to say nothing of daily conversation for customers."

Finally: "Foreign ladies can avail themselves of any desired hair style making during their stay in Japan, which causes them, we hope to find themselves more beautiful in case they return home."

Presumably, it goes without saying that you've

been made more beautiful, even if you don't return to your own country.

* * *

An advertisement for "Hearty Theater" says a musician "trapped the listeners in enchantment," and that the "line up of quest appearances is one that is not precedent."

A statement in a magazine says: "The most famous play of Agasa Christy is 'The Mouse Fred.'" No matter how hard you try—and I really did—it's nearly impossible to turn *The Mousetrap* into *The Mouse Fred*.

Next you come across a program for a concert that credits a performer as being "a companist." Is it a wonder that we turn to dictionaries ourselves?

Then there's an advertisement for an "Eye-filling strip show." There are four performances a day, and the advertisement asks that there be "No shifting of audience." All right, if you insist.

Another strip show, this one "De luxe," is open daily from noon to 11:30 P.M. The advertisement contains this friendly advice: "Beware of the talkers for such show."

A film synopsis of a long-ago movie, *A Countess From Hong Kong*, reads:

> As Ogden had too much to drink last night he cannot recall any incident that may explain Natascha's presence in his room. Although he is strongly attracted by her stunning beauty, he knows he cannot keep her forever as he realizes his important post as Ambassador to a Nation. Being afraid of a scandal, he tells Natascha to get out of his cabin room, threatening that he may call a purcer. She tells him that if he does such a thing, she will tear her dress with a scream, and will tell the purcer that Ogden was about to do violence to her.

A dilemma for any man, never mind an Ambassador to a Nation. However, as you might predict, all is satisfactorily resolved.

— 8 —
Wild Bore Soup

FROM EVERY DIRECTION come advertisements in Japanized English. A Tokyo restaurant attempts to lure customers via a magazine advertisement that reads in part:

> Why don't you try to present an extremely elegant dinner in this building, which was formally a baron's palace? . . . You may enjoy French dishes to your satisfaction in a fragrant noble atmosphere. On a cloudless day, it will be fine to have your meals under the shower of sunshine. You must spend a very happy time elated with a feeling as though you were in a scene of a high level movie drama of a love story.

Perhaps the same copywriter prepared the following on behalf of an eel restaurant. The flourish is similar. The advertisement says:

The building which was reconstructed in 1979 has dignified interior featured the color of black and we can feel its historical status in its modernity. Just looking at stone structure and black ceramics made by first-class artists, paper pictures, and all of decorated furniture, we become miraculously relazed and they give us complete fullness. This place is so popular that some people visit here three times a week. Not only the delicious eel that has ammothness and tastiness, but also its wonderful container placed various cookings fully utilized seasonal flavors are fascinating enough. They are using valuable tableware free from care. Their casual ways might be the luxury in real sense.

*　　*　　*

There's a coffee shop in Tokyo called "Mama's Fine Foods Desserts and Mind." Just the place to enjoy tea and cake dubbed "happy premonitions." Another coffee shop is named "Monkey Banana," while a third is "Cafe Tension."

A small restaurant christened itself "Perverse Person." That couldn't have happened solely by chance. Perhaps the owner asked a foreign friend to suggest a name, and the friend made a joke that was taken seriously.

A small curry shop is "Coffee and Curried," while a bar is "Telephone Clab Apple." A beer hall is

called "Hip Hop," while a hotel lounge is named "Face Off." There has to be a story there, too, although I'm not sure I want to hear it.

All around the large cities, towns, and resort areas of Japan thousands of restaurants, coffee shops, and bars vie for customers. To lure Westerners and other non-Japanese, many of these establishments provide menus in English, that is, in an English of sorts.

Here are a few items from the breakfast page of a hotel menu in a resort area. Start with a choice of "oreange" or "mix" juice. Next decide between "oots meal" and "corn frake." Eggs come "fread" or in the shape of an "Om Lat." If you have a sweet tooth, though, you might opt for "French Toost" or "Hot Coke." Decisions, decisions.

Some restaurants offer their food "buffer" style, others have specialties. A Chinese restaurant lists, among its lunchtime favorites, "steamed vegitable bums" and "steamed damplings."

Other restaurants, other specialties. One restaurant offers "cold condomme in dish." Kind of makes you splutter, doesn't it.

Follow it with "flying oil prawns," or an ordinary "hongbogo" (hamburger) or "good burger" sausage with "plan" rice. Or, if you prefer fish to meat, there are "fried flesh water shrimps."

Novel dishes from other menus include "fancy dog," "grilled winner," "dice beef steak," and "caab meet batter rice." The last one might sound more familiar as crab meat with buttered rice.

The more adventurous might consider "strawberry crap" for dessert. Well, as we know, a rose by any other name is still a rose. In this case, I hope that a crepe by any other name is still a crepe.

Let's not forget drinks to go with dinner. You can find "rose wine squash" on one menu, and "mucos" on another. Go right ahead if you like, but I'll stick with mineral water.

During the International Garden and Greenery Exposition, Osaka '90, also known as the Flower Expo, many signs in English popped up around the fairgrounds.

Restaurants, predictably, came up with memorable notices such as "When the crowded you get table in another parson."

Snack shops offered "Sofut cream," (soft ice cream) and "American dog." That's a good old-fashioned hot dog, although you've no doubt worked that out.

Visitors to the Expo were also said to have enjoyed "wild bore" soup and "see food."

To this day, a small neighborhood restaurant in a Tokyo suburb has this welcome in its window:

Notice! For All Foreign Lovable Visitors!
We all want to talk with you and hope you have a good time.

Such a charming greeting gives you a lift, whether or not you investigate further.

— 9 —
Horn Bread

A BREAD DELIVERY van has written on its side, in decisive letters: "Natural Bread and Delicious Life." Line up, all you health-food freaks.

A competitor goes a bit further. It markets its products in packages that say: "High nurient horn handmade bread. It's horn bread that is pursuing their purity."

Here's a third one to consider pursuing: "Hawaiian Pluck Bread."

Not too long ago, the Japanese were not very adventurous when it came to food. Rice and fish suited them fine, thank you very much. Just the smell of lamb cooking in the oven could send sensitive souls reeling out of the kitchen. Hot sauces and foreign spices were equally shunned.

Nowadays Japanese people fill Indian and other ethnic restaurants, eat hamburgers and french

fries, and clamor for pizza. Motor scooters delivering their orders nip through traffic and whiz around back streets. Pizza from one delivery company is free if it isn't in your hot little hands within thirty minutes of the time you called.

A step up on the home-delivery scale is a shop that delivers gourmet foods. It promises that "Under the motto of 'hand-prepared foods of fantastic flavor,' each and every one of our dishes is prepared with painstaking cars to offer you a delicious gourmet experience." And very nice it is, too.

*   *   *

Supermarket shelves overflow with packaged foods. On a day when you need to whip something up in a hurry, you might reach for ready-made hashed beef. It comes in a packet, with this to say for itself:

> GS foods has been studing a long time
> about what the best hashed beef taste shoud be.
> And here, proudly we are able to introduce
> our best hashed beef in retort packed
> which is everything
> that professional chef is going to season
> them are all done
> by just warm up our GS hashed beef.

Another instant product is soup, in a package that reads: "Finished a milk, if select the best material. Please pleasure a mild taste."

While you're "pouring" over the soups, so to speak, you might also consider "soup de corn" or "the goo." On the other hand "the goo" just might be one of life's little adventures best left untried.

A can of noodles advertises itself as a "Brand new light meal. The rule of Archimendes. Crispy tiny noodle × quality sauce = walking men i.e. Archimendes." Whatever you might say of copywriters in Japan, you must admire their creativity.

"Cheesen de Gourmet" is a cheese and Japanese cracker concoction. The message on its box proclaims the following:

Well-matched with Luxury. The recipe for CHEESEN here is deliberately chosen by The Ginza EDOICHI'S luxury; that will friendly put a spell over gourmets in tea and drinking time with his daring craft well-matched with its savor of ingredients as special and exclusive.

A baby-food company tells us that "Happy and fun snacks are said to bring up a gentle heart," and that "Even for eating habits, snacks during childhood cannot be disregarded. Please serve the Kewpie snack with mother's affectionate words." Mothers, take note.

Pet food also rates attention from copywriters. One particular dog food comes with this message:

> To tell the first, fresh meat is the best choice for your dog. Secondly, semi-moist dog food is it. So we add the naturiments: calcium, vitamins and many more. Because we are always thinking about the dogs' life through our semi-most dog foods since 1958.

> Nothing but the best for Fido, since 1958.

— 10 —
Selected Apples Born in Aomori

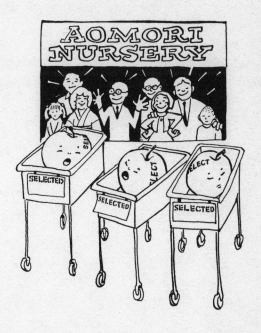

CANDY IS BIG business in Japan. In the back-to-frontness of the mysterious East, Valentine's Day has not been adopted for men to fuss over women, but rather for women to give men chocolate. This practice is not just limited to boyfriends and husbands. According to a recent questionnaire circulated among women in their twenties and thirties, the average modern Japanese miss gives chocolate to eight men on Valentine's Day. The men are colleagues and immediate superiors at work, as well as boyfriends, husbands, and other relatives. This translates into a staggering 37,200 tons of chocolates changing hands annually in the week before Valentine's Day.

Needless to say, chocolate boxes have messages on them, some as sizzling as "I will send him my hot heart dressed up to my heart's content on the day of love once a year."

There is a catch, however. It's not as though men can just accept their chocolates on February 14, and that's the end of it. They are expected to reciprocate.

One manufacturer even puts out Valentine's Day chocolates with this reminder on the box:

> With the sincerest feelings I present these sweet chocolates to you. But remember one thing, don't eat them all at once, but try to appreciate them one by one because they represent my feelings. Have the first piece today, have another tomorrow, and the day you have the last piece it will be your turn to give me a sweet White Day present.

The message is not very subtle. You see, March 14 has been set aside for men to give gifts in return. These gifts are not necessarily chocolates, either. The women answering the questionnaire said they'd accept anything, with preferences for jewelry and marriage proposals.

*   *   *

Yes, the sale of candy is serious business in Japan, and many a chocolate comes complete with lyrical phrases such as:

Happy Days.
A deliciousness born of a better idea and dedication to a better chocolate.

*Soft truffle smooth to melt in your mouth is wrapped
with milk chocolate.
Just try one, and light body and flavor will spread mildly,
so your heart echoes calmly.
This is a center-mix chocolate that holds fast
to be delicious.
Hearty present for anyone who loves genuine taste.*

Another company has this to say: "Four season is very hard to melt. It does not melt in your hand for 365 days." And then what? Could chocolate be programmed to disintegrate on the stroke of midnight, a year after leaving its factory? Do you suppose anyone ever tested the claim?

*   *   *

Shopping bags, too, carry "chocolatey" slogans. One says:

GRACEFUL CHOCOLATES

FANCY COLLECTION

*Chocolate was loved as luxury nourishment
by the princes and the noblement of
medieval Europe ever before.*

*This is the superb chocolate that has been
confectioned from the choice materials by using
the traditional technique of Switzerland.*

Lively Tea Time With Sweet Chocolates

Another bag takes a more direct approach: "Hi kids! Original Tastes a Lot of Licky! Chocolate Bar. How tiny, how light feelin'!! Kids of milk teeth and a grandma of artificial teeth can eat easy mind. Why? Because she isn't a hardrice criker. Of cause, OK for a man covered."

HI KIDS! ORIGINAL TASTES A LOT OF LICKY! How tiny, how light feelin'!! Kids of milk teeth and a grandma of art-ificial teeth can eat easy mind Why? Because she isn't a hardrice criker. Of cause, Ok for a man covered.

I was doing fine until I got lost between the "criker" and the "man covered."

* * *

A "Candy Pure Wine" is "refined candy made from pure wine brought up and ripened in the bosom of nature. Has delicate relish on the tongue and finely perfumes your mouth."

Another candy, "Milk Gummy" by name, invites you to "enjoy the heavenly aroma and tender sweet flavor of milk, enriched with calcium, in every lump of soft and creamy Milk Gummy."

"Milk Gummy" has a companion, "Grape Gummy." The wrapper rhapsodizes, "Enjoy the softness of gentle breeze that sweeps through the vineyard spread vast on the hill in each soft and juicy Grape Gummy." Let's hear it for the Gummy family!

Then there's "apple" candy, with its identification: "This candy is including fresh juice taken from selected apples born in Aomori. We can say it is almost raw apple." Almost, but not quite.

Another candy comes with these words:

> There are many tasty things in the world. Any new taste is a fad, but with time we go back to the original one. Because it is the real taste, Crunch candy 'Crundy' keeps the gourmet taste. It gives you the original flavor caring for small details in the material. When you chew it there's a light mellow feeling. It is an amusing buddy.

A shorter message, on yet another candy wrapper, invites you to "enjoy a relaxing Tart break, sitting by a bright window."

Finally, a "candy assort" comes in two flavors. The cherry and muscat has this conventional little ditty on the cover of the box: "The cherry is red, and the muscat grape is green, these candies are sweet, and so are you."

All quite innocuous, but "candy assort" should have stopped while it was ahead. For the message on the box of apple and lemon candy is slightly strange. It says: "The apple is luscious with dew, and the lemon is bright yellow from nature's bounty, and so are you."

—11—
I'm Dripper

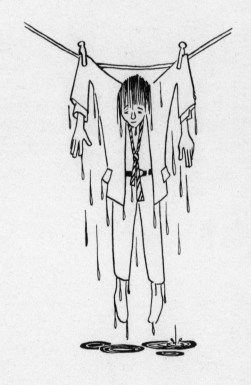

IT WOULD BE difficult to be thirsty for long in Japan. Products on supermarket shelves run the gamut from the softest of juice to the hardest of alcohol. Neighborhood shops carry most of the essentials. Vending machines stock beer as well as vast quantities of soft drinks. And most of these vending machines, aside from being omnipresent, stay on all night.

The slogans that appear on bottled drinks often resemble those that appear on candy wrappers. For instance, a fruit drink says on its bottle: "Enjoy this refreshment of the sparkling raspberry taste for your precious time." There's something very familiar about that.

The message goes on to say: "Enjoy the sparkling and refreshing taste of fizzwater made of nature-refined quality water to the full." Fizzwater must be bubbly mineral water, and a particularly healthy one at that. Or so its manufacturers would have us believe.

An eloquent message carried on a Japanese beer can says: "Just as the best malts, hops and other ingredients are native to the northern climes, so does the Northern Star shine on this custom-brewed, limited-run edition bring you the bracing taste of Hokkaido's rustic flavor." Long may the Northern Star shine on the limited-run edition.

The statement on an apple-juice carton says: "A variety of fresh fruit juice obtained through abundant use of rich foreign-grown fruits. 100%

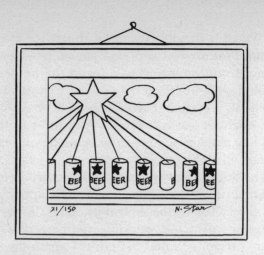

21/150   N. Star

pure and natural with vivid savor of raw materials."
Put simply, and in fewer words, it's the real thing!

* * *

Coffee is surprisingly good here in this land of
green tea. There's always plenty to read on the
packages as you select your brand. If instant is your
blend, consider "I'm Dripper," an instant-coffee
powder sold in plastic containers. Just add hot
water, mix, and you too can be a dripper.

One canned coffee, a vending-machine special,
is called "Old Beans." Another is called "Jaguar." It
comes in a jar with two words on it: "critical drip."
Maybe Jaguar meets even the harshest critic's
standards. Or perhaps even the most critical enjoy
it to the last drip.

Another coffee claims that it is "solely for the refined adult people." Instant disqualification for many potential customers.

A lengthier advertisement has this to say for its product:

It's happiness people loving casual true caring friends taste everyday relaxing coziness fun intimate hot open likeable and togetherness. It's warmth honest embracing pure gentle comradship you family us sharing sociable aroma liveliness tenderness smiling easy and yours.

That's a lot for one little coffee to live up to.

*   *   *

Each day, at regular intervals, the American armed forces radio station in Japan, the Far East Network, gives us the weather outlook. Often, the report ends with: "The weather is a courtesy of your local oceanographic and weather station." Am I the only person who winces at this?

Some time ago a Japanese cosmetics company came out with a slogan that sparked a furor in the foreign community in Tokyo. The slogan was: "For beautiful human life." For a spell, people wrote letters to the editor of a daily English-language newspaper in Tokyo, simply to argue the meaning of the phrase. Yet I've never heard anyone so much

as comment on the weather itself coming to us courtesy of our local oceanographic and weather station.

Such big-name stars as James Coburn and Roger Moore rake in the money advertising a Japanese brand of cigarettes called Lark. I wonder what, if anything, they think of the punch line of their television commercial. It is, simply, "Speak Lark." Seems to be at least as inappropriate as "For beautiful human life," yet it's accepted without comment, as is Coca-Cola's maxim, "I feel Coke."

The advertisement "All season taste great—live beer for live people" confounds some folk. After all, we don't drink seasons, and who but live people would be drinking beer, be it live or not?

I have a nomination, should prizes ever be handed out in Japan for "most extraordinary advertisement in the category of food and drink." It is "World's finest whiskey made from Scotland's finest grapes."

— 1 2 —
The Shortened History of Mankind

LIVING IN JAPAN brings out the collector in many a foreigner, for Japanese treasures fit snugly and happily into Western homes.

Some collectibles are *tansu,* the beautiful wooden chests-of-drawers; *hibachi,* the old-style fire pots in wood or porcelain; and *netsuke,* the exquisite miniature ivory carvings. Traditionally, *netsuke* were attached to gentlemen's tobacco pouches or medicine boxes, and portrayed many aspects of life in Japan. Today, collectors simply arrange them on display shelves. Other favorite items of Japanalia include woodblock prints, screens, and fans. You can also find lacquerware, porcelain, and ceramics, not to mention teapots, baskets, and folk crafts.

Just for fun, some foreigners also collect shopping bags with weird messages in English. "I will do human life," for instance.

Perhaps the author of that phrase dreamed up the cosmetic company's "For beautiful human life" logo, as well as the beer company's "Live beer for live people." Or maybe the writers just graduated from the same school?

Other shopping bags sport such garbled messages as "London XYZ. All those floodlights spin your head around. Dance and prance across the stage shaking things in a peculiar way."

A bag from a sports-equipment store says: "Serve the athletes. Nike and Swoosh." Do you wear "Swoosh" on your feet, too?

Here are a few more nutty messages seen on shopping bags:

Fatty Don, the fish with the turned down eyes.

Fruit Panic.

In the southern island of children go to sea.

Four monkeys get hold on tight to edge of boat not to fall down.

Pee Wee Bear, he is a popular person can't sit down.

Reverge. The best things in life are free. Though regret. Lovely Fruits basket. The Sweet Fruits Have Experience of Faint First Love.

A single sound can freshen up my tired heart without fail to me. Sound is the most important of all arts.

Chatterbox. Happiness is Visiting Little World.

A Stage in Life. Gentle Hippo and His Beautiful Girl Friend.

* * *

Although I try to minimize my quoting of vulgarity, there is certainly plenty of it around, most of which, I think and hope, finds its way into print inadvertently. The Nebstar shopping bag, for instance. Written on it is the eye-catching, "F . . . THE NEBSTAR BABIES WHILE YOU CAN." The deleted version is mine. The bag has the word written out in its entirety, in big, bold, capital letters.

The copy says—and I faithfully reproduce the punctuation and spelling—"In the world we're gonna have no more f...ing luxary yes, it's good thing to realize that it's up to 'heart' now, only Nebstar can five you the way it feel it in you can see these 'Nebstar Babies' are inface one girl yeah, you know that girl always wants some more feeling sorry that we can not stop it—it is a kind of nature."

A series of rather arty-looking fashion sketches, each separately labeled, further compounds the Nebstar mystery. The labels say: "Ms Do-Yourself, Ms Rip-Me-Off, Ms Space-Out, Ms Get High, Ms Be-A-Man, Ms Chase-Me, Ms Take-Out, Ms Thrill-Me, Ms Stone-Free, Ms I-Need-It and Ms Take-Easy."

All this Nebstar nonsense was, at one time, beautifully printed on large shopping bags in an assortment of colors, and sold in a reputable shop. No one quite knew who or what Nebstar was, nor what the bag was trying to say. However, could a company with the motto "We feel for people, people feel for us" be all bad?

* * *

Writing paper in Japan is another rich source of strange English. A manufacturer called "Tabasco Family" puts out a writing pad with "S . . . " written on it. Again, the dots are mine, the writing pad has no inhibitions.

The drawing portrays two characters who look as if they've stepped out of a "Far Side" cartoon. One is a masked hippopotamus with a sack slung over its shoulder. The other character is a policeman, although you'd be hard put to identify him as such, in his long coat and tie with a hat hiding his face.

The message, after "S . . . ," goes on to say:

> Oh, My God! That ain't cool, man. How come this guy is always sticking around. Can't get rid of it. See, I can't survive if I don't do my business. What's wrong with taking some tiny things from the richy. What a hell!!

What a message!

Shorter messages on stationery include:

The Shortened History of Mankind.
How many people I wonder will keep being so
   pure minded as a white cloud in the sky?
Pastel emotions for tender moods, a pastel
   feeling between us, too. Pastel bonds forever
   true.

A notebook cover has this to say for itself:

Favorite stories, interesting stories, all kinds of
stories for dreamers everywhere a long, longed-
for land. It is cold tonight, really cold. On nights
like these, we are responsible for taking care of
the castle. Do you suppose some troublemaker
will show up? Perhaps a mischievous fire-
breathing dragon may come to attack us. As we
all worry about things like this, we make our
rounds over the castle grounds.

—13—
Fitty Shoes

WEARING JACKETS AND jerseys, T-shirts and sweaters with English words and phrases on them has long been in vogue in Japan. Clothing manufacturers and retailers admit that they themselves don't necessarily know what they say. Anyway, they shrug, it's not the words that matter, no one ever asks what they mean. It's the colors and designs that sell.

Well, occasionally a phrase makes sense. "Half a Loaf is better than None a Loaf," for example.

And the phrase "woker's holic" concisely sums up Japan's reputation in the world.

More often than not, though, the words on clothing have little meaning, even when only one, two, or three words are involved. "Fancy pimple," for instance. Or "Molded Fish," "Funny Kilt Clan," "Bull Head," and "Shorty Shiner."

Perhaps you'd rather wear one of those than a jacket with a picture of a bicycle and these three understandable words: "Between your legs." Or perhaps a plain white T-shirt with "Murderer" in black letters. Or a shirt that says "Throw up."

Would you wear a sweatshirt that says "Just Fit to You. King Kong"? Or one that says "Porky Party"?

Even wilder is this slogan on a pair of overalls. Under a drawing of a pig are the words "Drug Store Body. Let's get the Good Shape and have a sexy body just like a pig." Wait a minute. Just what is going on around here?

*　　*　　*

Here are a few slogans seen on clothes around the streets of Tokyo:

Just say no to socks.

God save the Cecilia.

Fresh communication by fruit: Fresh Kiss.

Have a relish for amenity expression.

Scandal scoop. Collection: Milk Pot. Heart Beat Zip.

To touch a boy's adventurous brain, dream and inquisity.

It's natural that we should love with this members.

This Clothes Offered Cries of Joy and Happiness as it Stood Up.

Flawless World. We have created the space that is worse trying.

A Basic Gear Old Status Men's Clothe. Dries nail polish, stockings or paint. Defrosts refrigerators. Has dozens of home uses.

"BASSETT WALKER" Go ahead, make my Tag. The Dawning of a New Age.

For Old College Members. Attack the Chance. Reveal Your True Self. We Wearing Nice Clothes By Yourself.

Daring Spirit. Japanese man have a this spirit all TIME since ancient.

EXERCISE FOR KIDS! Breaking generation 'On-Air' Permanet Charm. None of your impudence.

* * *

There's often more to read on people than is possible as they walk past you. You would have to share a train journey, at least, to be able to read all of this:

Ladies and Gentlemen. Let me introduce a long-awaited our new friend. It is very lovely

news this way, please hello everybody. How do you do we call 'Tero' hysteric glamor obscene art projects. Nice to meet you. I want to make friends with you. You feel the time of miserable, joyful at all times, beside of you, but be careful. I'm a dangerous put the noticeable place.

Here is a slogan so convoluted that you wonder who could have concocted it, and why: "Frais es pec. Formidable the rising era. Be indignant. Perplaxity. Be amazed. A CHARACTRISTIC Tec. 1: a ffected. Tec 2: a prank. Tec 3: showy. Tec 4: a shrewd. Tec 5: cool-headed. Tec 6: be single-minded."

Some messages become even stranger than they already are because of the unorthodox hyphenation of words. For instance:

PROLOOK both study and sport are important, this for the dev-elopment of the body an-d that for the improveme-nt of the mind sports.

A men's suit—not a unisex one but a proper men's suit—has a discreet label sewn into the inside pocket. "Bust size M," it says.

Women's underwear, manufactured in Japan under license from the American company Fruit of the Loom, adds a second little tag to accompany the Fruit of the Loom label. It says: "Fruity joy, refined sense." Now you are properly dressed, so to speak, and ready to face the world.

Meanwhile, a card attached to a scarf reads: "Original Gift. Fashion collection for you with Simple Mind. Natural life and Simple Mind. May you be happy. And may you be young." And may you be bright enough to work all of that out!

Blue jeans might feel incomplete without a card to escort them to their new home. The card says: "Wonder quantity and feeling. Always stimulative and so sensitive commodities. As Every Stitch Has Been Done Cautiously, You Can Get More Brilliant Looking When You Put On This Garment." Who could possibly resist such a sales pitch?

It is certainly a cut above this advertisement:

Fashion Mongers Goes Next Trendy 1988–89. We want clothing wave. Under the serious consideration, interest one-new-style, read to be casual and self in stylish. NAVY, PUNK and more: Beyond description. To be continue!

However, it seemed to be so far beyond description that it never continued.

Some people attach medals and badges to their clothes, presumably to add a military touch. That is to say they attach "medals and punkish budges." The look they achieve is most certainly different.

At least one department store in Tokyo has a section that sells "shirts and blows," while another offers "fooded blousons." What's more, a Japanese shoe maker sells "fitty shoes." That's good news for those of us who don't have dainty Cinderella feet. We won't have to stock up in our own countries anymore, not if we can find shoes that "fitty" right here in Japan.

—14—
Avoid the Wind
from Flowers

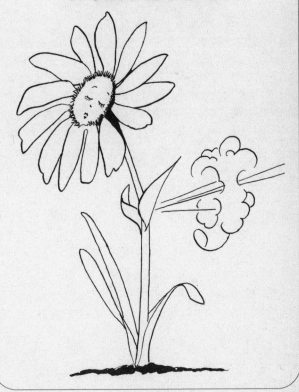

AS LANGUAGE STUDENTS often moan, asking carefully memorized questions in a foreign tongue and actually understanding the replies are two entirely different matters. If only people whom you ask these carefully memorized questions would spout the same sort of carefully memorized textbook responses!

Fast-food chains in Japan have their employees learn a few phrases in English so they can communicate with foreigners. Just a few basic words to smooth the transaction of money for food.

So, when the Englishman places his order at Kentucky Fried Chicken, the girl behind the counter doesn't miss a beat. Perhaps she doesn't even listen to his order, so intent is she on trotting out the phrase she has carefully memorized.

"Eat here or take out?" she asks.

She is completely unprepared for the expression of rage on the Englishman's face. He is incensed by her question.

He has just asked for four barrels of chicken and twenty orders of french fries and coleslaw. Now really. Does the girl behind the counter honestly think he's going to sit down and polish all of that off by himself?

We are constantly reminded in Japan that a little language goes a long way. Now and then, however, it can also go the wrong way.

*　　*　　*

English is such a tiresome language. It's as if it's forever lying in wait to trip you up on the smallest details. It just doesn't seem fair that the difference of a single letter should change something straightforward into something indecent.

For instance, the Japanese staff of a Western club in Tokyo prepares labels to identify the work displayed in a needlework exhibition. They create an unintentional sensation by dropping an innocent little *o* from a word. The exhibit in question shows "counted stitch work." Instead, well, the harmless little *o* isn't deleted from "work." It is dropped from "counted." The needlework exhibition attracts many more people than it has anticipated, and, as word spreads, viewers arrive with cameras.

"They'll never believe this back home," they say to each other.

Furthermore, a Japanese secretary working for an international firm almost unhinges an American

man when she politely asks him, "May I have your office telephone number and your privates?"

✳ ✳ ✳

Although there's no denying the national confusion in Japan over *l*'s and *r*'s, not every *l*, written or oral, automatically turns into an *r*. Instead, they are interchanged quite haphazardly.

For example, a T-shirt says "frip-flap," a menu says "french flies," and a shop sells "letter lacks." A travel agency promotes a "plum brossom" viewing expedition.

A printer, putting out the membership roster of a local organization, sends the following request: "We are sending the proof you ordered. Please ploof read the said proof and return the same to us soonest possible so that we can proceed next steps."

"Ploof the proof." Curious, isn't it? Yet consistent enough to warrant comment.

Still, more often than not, *l*'s turn into *r*'s and vice versa. A sign in the park points the way to the "ravatoli." The delivery van of a florist says "frolist" on the side.

An invitation arrives in the mail for the "gara performance" of a ballet. The theme music for a television program is credited to "Henly Mancini."

Even after reaching the stage of automatically transposing *l*'s and *r*'s you still might blink at the menu for a traditional Japanese dinner. There it is, in black and white: "law eggs" and "lice."

That pales in significance when compared to the referral to the future emperor of Japan as the "clown prince." This is a mistake that has crept into print, as well as into speech, more than once.

Even worse, though, is the experience of an American going to his first Japanese memorial service. He knows that he is expected to join the line of mourners, pick up a white chrysanthemum,

and place it by the photograph of the deceased. He also knows that he should clap his hands. He has worked this out from a note slipped to him by a Japanese colleague.

The note says: "To show respect for the deceased, approach his picture and crap three times."

*　　*　　*

Abbreviations open up whole new dimensions in language pitfalls. Many years ago a Tokyo International Trade Fair employed a bevy of attractive young women to act as guides. Each woman's uniform came complete with a badge that said "TIT FAIR." Needless to say, the badges didn't last the run of the fair. As soon as the meaning was pointed out, the badges were hastily withdrawn.

Nor is the spoken word safe from potential disaster. More than one speaker at a luncheon or dinner in the East has found himself introduced as an "extinguished speaker."

A dignified Japanese gentleman at a black-tie charity dinner once concluded his speech in English with these profound words: "I would like to thank you from the heart of my bottom."

*   *   *

After all of that, you can take in stride the written statement "avoid the wind from flowers." A friend receives a flower arrangement that arrives with instructions for enjoying them for "long days." It stresses that flowers should be watered daily and looked after with "warm support." The instruction "avoid the wind from flowers" is clarified with "please take care to prevent flowers from direct wind of air conditioners."

A sports club in Tokyo circularizes a letter to members, enclosing car stickers for the next fiscal year. The letter concludes: "Please discard your old sticker at your end." One member wonders if the club means the old sticker should be discarded at his demise. "Or do you suppose they have something more sinister in mind?" he asks.

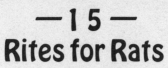

—15—
Rites for Rats

MUCH OF THE local news that is reported in Tokyo's English-language newspapers comes from the vernacular press. Perhaps translation is responsible for the amazing blandness of some reports.

A headline of yesteryear reads: "Tanaka Secretly Took 90 Minute Car Ride." The story begins: "Former Prime Minister Kakuei Tanaka, who is now recovering from a stroke he suffered last February, last month slipped out of his home for a car ride of about 90 minutes in Tokyo, sources close to Tanaka disclosed Thursday."

The story elaborates on the former politician's recovery from his stroke, and concludes triumphantly: "He is getting better fast enough to go out in a car, the sources said."

* * *

Some stories take your breath away. For instance this tale about a thief, Ito by name, who specializes in stealing items from parked vehicles, and keeps his victims' driver's licenses as a record of his work.

After three hundred thefts, the police find 181 driver's licenses, 47 credit cards, and 90 purses and wallets in his room.

The newspaper account says: "Asked why he had kept such evidence, Ito said another thief had told him that he was scolded by detectives because he could not remember details of his many crimes. Ito kept a diary of his thefts for about three months after he first became a thief, but the diary was stolen by another burglar. Ito then decided to keep licenses. Questioned by police, Ito easily gave the dates of the crimes when he was shown the licenses." And perhaps his conscientious record keeping is taken into account when he is sentenced.

Another item tells of three masked men who break into the house of some eel-keepers, bind and gag them, then proceed to net fifty thousand eels. The story continues: "The thieves also took 30 bags of eel food, containing 20 kilograms each, to cap their six hours of work." Those men may never have worked quite so hard, nor with such concentration, as they did that night.

Another break-in story tells of two men who enter a house and "tie up a 13-year-old boy who was alone in the house with tape." Poor lad! He's quietly watching television in the "loving room" when he is suddenly assaulted. Still, he does live to tell about it.

Another newspaper story tells of a hit-and-run accident that ends with several injuries and one death. The newspaper concludes that "Police later found a suspicious car in a vacant lot." We are left in

suspense, though, never being told whether or not they arrest the offending car.

I read another account of a different crime where a suspect was "arrested red-handed."

The following notice was written in Japanese, not in Japanized English, but I am taking the liberty of translating it. It was posted on an impressive building on a busy Tokyo street. In large letters it commanded: "Absolutely no burglars beyond this point."

*　　*　　*

A newspaper story tells us that a Tokyo radio station is offering children the chance to plant rice in a "muddy puddy."

A television guide in a newspaper gives a film synopsis. The film revolves around a "gusty" woman in a trade union.

Another television guide has a picture of a

Japanese actress sitting with several robed and turbanned men. The explanation tells us that she "visits a camel market in Egypt where humorous camels are bought and sold three times a week."

Those camels might have had quite a chuckle over this next news item. It begins:

> A university professor of bacteriology was shot and injured being mistaken for a rabbit by a hunter, while collecting wild mushrooms in a forest in Yamagata Prefecture Monday afternoon.

The story goes on to say that the police are questioning the hunter on suspicion of professional negligence resulting in injury, and ends: "Investigators suspect that the hunter shot the professor at about 50 meters' distance, taking him for a rabbit." Talk of adding insult to injury. It's bad enough to be shot by accident, but because you've been mistaken for a rabbit?

* * *

Where else but Japan would a story like this appear in the newspaper? It says that the Ministry of Health and Welfare will "set stern sanitary standards for hand towels." It appears that some used *oshibori*, the ubiquitous towels provided by restaurants, sit for days before being washed. And while they sit, bacteria and germs proliferate. However, rest assured, because "The Ministry plans to set a standard of just how many germs per towel will be acceptable." I've been waiting to know the answer for years, but it has never been announced.

"Rites for Rats" is the headline of a news story which goes on to say:

About thirty solemn-faced Sanitation Department officials got together recently for a religious service—for dead cockroaches, mosquitoes, flies and rats. Before an altar, a Shinto priest prayed for a 'quiet repose to the soul of these insects and animals. If you are ever reborn, we pray that it will be as something that will do good to people.'

Prayers out of the way, and consciences eased, the sanitation officials settle down to the rest of their meeting. They are assembled to discuss methods for exterminating cockroaches, mosquitoes, flies, and rats.

— 1 6 —
Cuddle Puddle

BY NO MEANS does Japan have a monopoly on mangled English. Howlers pop up all over the world, even in countries where English is the national language. Sometimes, of course, laughs are deliberately being courted.

Somebody, or several somebodies, must have enjoyed composing this sign posted near an elevator in Hong Kong. It says: "Going up, press UP. Going down, press DOWN. Pressing both together get you nowhere. In fact, quicker to walk."

Most signs mean only to instruct and inform. Some of them cause laughter which is unintentional, but then, of course, different things strike different people as being funny.

It's hard for me to keep a straight face when confronted with signs such as this one in Bali:

You must be well dressed on the road. Violating this rule you will be seized and confiscated.

Or this notice in a Kampuchean hotel, when the country was still Cambodia: "We beg our customers not to circulate in bathing suits."

*   *   *

Hotels the world over have rules and regulations. A backpackers' hotel in Tanzania posts this sign in its lobby: "No lady of moral turpitude shall be allowed to enter the premises."

Scrutinized and admitted, you then find this

notice in your room: "Clients are requested not to put friendship and trust whilst they are away in the bathroom. All residents are requested to live in harmone and peace."

A hotel in French Guiana has a notice in its guest rooms that warns: "The use of electric irons in the guest is not permitted." The very idea!

A European hotel asks its guests to "Please walk carefully, talk low, and reduce noise of transistors to the maximum."

This puzzling notice was once attached to a tree in Olympia, Greece: "Washing of cars forbidden." You really can't help but wonder why.

A visitor to the Canary Islands exclaims at the information that buses run "every hour at half past the hour, give or take 30 minutes."

The visitor to Zambia enjoys a road sign that warns drivers of "Uncontrolled pedestrians crossing ahead."

A letter from an Indian travel agent solemnly confirms our "births" on a train journey around the subcontinent. No denying that "berth" and "birth" sound precisely the same, but still . . .

Sometimes the letter order in words gets rearranged. A company in Sumatra offers a line of "welcome" mats, that is to say, it offers a line of "melcowe" mats.

Billiards seems to be popular in some Sumatran towns. One up-to-date establishment has "Bill Yard" written across its door. A long-distance bus in Sumatra brags on its brochure that it has deluxe "recleaning" seats.

Sometimes you doubt your ears as well as your eyes. Surely the stewardess on an Asian airline couldn't have just said: "In a few minutes we will have the pleasure of serving you a Frenchman." No, she must have said refreshment.

Could another flight attendant, on another Asian carrier, really have said: "In case of sudden loss of pleasure in the cabin, oxygen masks will automatically descend. Please put your oxygen mask over your mouse"? No, you must have misheard.

*   *   *

A hotel in Korea provides toothbrushes for its guests. They come in cardboard boxes labeled "Tooth and Brush."

In Taiwan you go to your local "beauty talon" for a manicure, as well as "hair-dressing."

A Thai shop, selling tennis and jogging outfits, has a sign in its window that says "sport swear."

A fitting room in an Indian dress shop calls itself a "trial room," while a shop in Kenya sells "shoes and slappers," to say nothing of "shots and trousers."

In several Asian countries, people have personal

seals which they use to stamp documents, instead of signing them. Although seals are registered, anyone can have one made, and losing yours can be more serious than losing a credit card.

Should you be interested in having a seal made, there's a shop in Hong Kong waiting to make it for you. It is called "Chops Craving."

*　　*　　*

A cafe in Bali offers a breakfast special of "toes with butter and jam." A menu in Thailand features "coconut mile" under drinks, and "scrab" under seafood. You can top it off with a dessert of "banana flitters" or "ice cream boomed Alaska."

A restaurant in Malaysia is called "Soon Go Fatt." It should join forces with the hotel in Sri Lanka that offers an "a la crate" menu.

A restaurant in Vietnam specializes in "pork with fresh garbage." Relax, the cabbage is perfectly edible.

Menus in Sumatra offer appalling-sounding dishes such as "bawels in cow sauce." Bars are "well-socked" with such drinks as "sour sop juice," "coffee and egg," "green sand bottle," and "green sand tin." Cheers!

A shop in Grenada says that it is "licensed to sell spirituous liquor."

A menu in Nepal offers "patched eggs" and "muddle chicken with finger cheep." Another version of chicken, this one unmuddled, comes with "battle green gourd." Another dish is "half fried." That's all, just your everyday half fried. Or perhaps you'd prefer "fried friendship"?

Meanwhile, in Africa, you might live on "dirty rice," "klippers," and "fat cakes." In Ghana you can buy a hotly spiced pepper sauce. It comes in a tin, with the ingredients properly listed: "pepper, shrimps, ginger, fish, tomatoes, natural spices, vegetable oil and preservatives." The sauce is called "Shitto."

*　*　*

A brochure for a Madeira hotel assures its guests that "comfort and kindness scents each atmosphere of an arrival." That's nice to know when you turn up jet lagged and grubby.

A tourist pamphlet lauding Madeira wines contains this bewildering information: "The special climate and soil so improved the original qualities of the vine and the island wines gained such fame that in 1478 the Duck of Clarence, brother of King Edward IV of England drowned in a vat of Malmsey." You puzzle over that for a while. Why should the Duke of Clarence—at least you realize he is a Duke and not a duck—drown in a vat of Malmsey because the wine was famous?

Then you come across another brochure which clarifies the mystery. It says that in the first half of

the fifteenth century Madeira wine achieved international renown. "Not only did ladies use Madeira wine to perfume their handkerchiefs, but the Duke of Clarence, condemned to death by the House of Lords, chose, as the means of his execution, to be drowned in a cask of Malvasia." What a way to go!

*　　*　　*

Did you know that there are hot springs in Swaziland, a tiny country sandwiched between South Africa and Mozambique? You'd be hard put, though, to identify them on a local brochure. They're called "cuddle puddles."

Taiwan has, or at least once upon a time had, a "Happy VD Clinic." Hard to believe—the happy part, I mean.

The next sign once adorned a wooden building in Korea. The year was 1953. An armistice had been signed ending the Korean War, and certain steps were being taken to change Korea's image.

This sign said it all: "We No More Whorehouse. Now Number 1 Laundry. You Still Come Please."

*　　*　　*

Personally, I think the world is richer for the howlers that creep into print. There's nothing like a good laugh to help you through a day, any day, not just a difficult one. Here are a few headlines that local English-language newspapers have printed over the years:

Solution to Laotian Crisis Unsolved
Review Definition of Death, Body Advises
Soy Sauce Killer Arrested by Police
Ban Love Hotels Move
Tokyu Hands Holding Contest
Thai Meatball Maker Declines Vasectomy
Police Grill Three Over Fraudulent Cook Pot Sales
Police Grill Hostess Over Burned Body Case
Democrats Carve Each Other Up in Debate Before First Key Primary
Dole Poised To Burn Bush in Iowa
Violence, Dark Horse Surge in Peru Election Race
Change in Executing Editor
One Out of Every Japanese Is Ill
Nurse Dies From Deadly Prick
Asian Money Ducks for Cover as Gulf War Looms

A photograph in a local newspaper showed former Prime Minister Noboru Takeshita and his wife departing for an overseas trip. The caption read: "Prime Minister Noboru Takeshita waves his hand along with his wife Naoko, Tuesday morning." Now there's a strong man for you!

A headline in the overseas page of a local newspaper in the United States said: "Police Kill Man to Stop His Attempt at Suicide." The story elaborated that police in the Philippines shot a man who was poised to jump off the roof of a building. They shot him to prevent him from killing himself, according to the story.

A typographical error from a long-ago report in *The Times* of London must have amused its readers. Apparently Queen Victoria "passed over" Westminster Bridge en route to a royal engagement somewhere in London. As ordinary a court circular as ever was printed. However, in the typesetting of the sentence, the *a* of "passed" turned into an *i*. No one in the newspaper office noticed the gaffe until after the papers had hit the newsstands.

Although nobody noticed this mistake until it was too late to correct it, an edition of a children's Bible was printed in Hong Kong and sent out into the world with a title page that read: "With a foreword Archie, the Bishop of Canterbury."

The Archbishop of Canterbury at the time was Dr. Runcie. When he visited Japan in 1987, the Japanese came up with yet another version of his title. On May 12, 1987, a huge welcome banner was raised across the street in front of St. Paul's University, Tokyo. It said in bold, black letters: "WELCOME RUNCIE THE, ARCHBISHOP OF CANTERBURY." No doubt Dr. Runcie just took the greeting in stride.

*　　*　　*

Even the BBC, a standard for correct English, has been guilty of misplacing the occasional phrase. An educational broadcast once informed us that "the Concorde was the first plane to carry passengers eating their dinner at twice the speed of sound." No wonder the press was alerted. That's an achievement worthy of a worldwide news flash.

One morning the American armed forces radio news-announcer in Tokyo said, "After being artificially inseminated, zookeepers say Ling-Ling is now exhibiting proper nesting behavior." Unfortunately there has never been a follow-up on that fascinating snippet of information about the lives of zookeepers and pandas.

Sports commentators, in the excitement of the moment, come up with their share of magnificent bloopers. For example, from an English radio broadcast comes this puzzling sentence: "He kicked the ball with his favorite left leg."

Other anatomically incorrect comments note that "The manager is in the happy position of having a fresh pair of legs up his sleeve," and "Not enough of our players in England are two-footed."

An advertisement in an American newspaper said: "Fried chicken prepared while you wait in the old iron skillet." It must have been an iron skillet of gigantic proportions.

Meanwhile, a newsletter from a small English village mentioned a summer party that was "held in a shady councillor's garden."

The following sentence came from the program of an English-language amateur dramatic organization, and was written by an Englishman. No excuses for him! He wrote: "An encouraging feature of this season has been the steady flow of new blood on the stage."

Another program put out by the same group, perhaps written by the same volunteer, contained this biographical item: "He evidently enjoyed the role of stage manager in our last presentation since he is back in the saddle and is finding time for an acting part to boot."

A recent newsletter of a Western club in Tokyo—yes, written by a native speaker—said that "Complaints have been received that there are loose stools around the bar. The Catering Committee has referred them to the Interior Committee." Let's hope the Interior Committee took some action!

Believe me, I'm not poking fun at those who make mistakes in what is not their "mum tongue," as an Indian girl calls her first language. We're all guilty!

*　　*　　*

There are times when messages written in the clearest of English still cause confusion. A contact-lens wearer needed to clean her lenses in hot water each night. She usually carries a little machine with her when she travels from America to Europe, but on one memorable occasion she forgot to take an adapter for European voltage.

On her first night in Ireland, she wrote a note that said: "Please boil these for 10 minutes with the eggs." She put the note and the contacts in an envelope which she placed with the breakfast order outside the door of the hotel room.

The waiter who brought the room-service breakfast the next morning carried in the contact lenses in their own bowl of hot water. He carefully scooped them out with tongs and deposited them on a plate on the breakfast table. If he thought that some people ate very strange things for breakfast, his expression didn't give him away.

We all have our moments. I remember a British businessman in Tokyo who emerged rather shakily from a long, intense business meeting.

"I need a drink," he said. "For a moment there, I really thought it was carpets for me."